Vegetarian
The Taste of South India

Vegetarian
The Taste of South India

Photography & Concept: Salim Pushpanath

Recipe: Manju Rahim

Food Stylist: Rasheed Muhammed Oliyantakath

Photography associated: Lenin S Lankayil

The brands used for the Food Presentation in this book are
MITTERTEICH, MODERNE & AVANTGARDE, represented all
over India by INTERMARKETING - imtablewares@gmail.com.
Distributed in Kerala exclusively through JNB Marketing India
Pvt Ltd - jnb@ricmail.com

For overseas rights and sales,
please contact the publisher

Published by Salim Pushpanath
DEE BEE INFO PUBLICATIONS
"Pushpanath", Malloossery,
Kottayam - 686 041, Kerala, India.
Tel: 91 481 2391429,2302799,91 9447043259
Email: salimpushpanath@gmail.com
www.salimpushpanath.com

Printed in Malaysia

ISBN 978-81-88000-30-2
Price: Rs.395/-

Recipe **Manju Rahim**

Contents

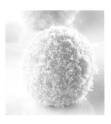

Introduction

The popularity of South Indian food was born out of the ever-increasing number of South Indian restaurants around the world and the rise in popularity of South India as a tourist destination. Vegetarian cooking in this region has continued for centuries and its simplicity and health benefits are discussed widely not only in India but around the world.

South India is very diverse in culture, customs and language. But one common factor that binds it together is the vegetarian cuisine that is very popular in this region. The common perception that vegetarian cuisine does not offer a very wide choice of dishes is largely false, as can be seen by the countless and mind boggling number of dishes available in this very small region of India alone.

The food in South India varies regionally, with each state having its unique dishes as well as its own variation of similar recipes, each with their own traditional blend of spices and ingredients.

Though each of the South Indian states has its own typical vegetarian dishes, many dishes are common across the region. *Dosa, idli, uthappam, rasam, sambar* and *chutney* are some of the many traditional dishes that are consistent throughout the region.
Each dish has many varieties, and each version brings out the taste of each state. As a result, putting together a book on the vast varieties of South Indian vegetarian cuisine was a very challenging task.

I have tried to choose the recipes in this book to reflect an ideal cross section of dishes representative of the region, and very carefully selected them to bring in the best on board.

I was always fascinated with home cooking and I learned traditional South Indian cooking techniques and spice blends from my mother. Watching her cook traditional recipes has taught me a lot, which I have tried to include in this book. Even though I am living abroad with my family, I still practice the old fashioned South Indian way of cooking, which has been passed down for generations. I like to follow traditional recipes but in a simplified fashion, adapted to our busy modern lives and kitchens.

The recipes in this book originate from the South Indian states of Kerala, Tamil Nadu and Karnataka. In Kerala, cooking is mostly coconut based – coconut oil is used as a cooking medium and the white core is grated and ground to a paste with spices, and the delicious coconut milk is extracted and added to curries like beetroot curry in coconut milk.
Tamil Nadu cuisine is famous for its spicy but simple flavours like *Thakkali kothamalli rasam* and *Sambar*. Karnataka cuisine is unique with its spice blends and flavour combinations, such as *Puliyogare* and *Bisi bele bath*.

The recipes in this book are chosen in such a way that they are easy to replicate using ingredients available all around the world. Some of the specific ingredients that may not be easily available outside India may be substituted with local ingredients without compromising the authentic taste. I have added these suggestions in the recipes, but other adaptations can also be made, according to your own taste.

The overriding attractions of south Indian cuisine are the textures, flavours, overwhelming aroma of spices and the sourness of tamarind pulp.
The food in South India is at its glorious best in the individual local homes, where it is mostly cooked by following the traditional recipes and using the local ingredients. But the availability of spices and exotic ingredients around the world makes south Indian cuisine accessible to all and thus makes it one of the most exciting new trends in the culinary world.
I hope you will have fun cooking these recipes and be inspired to try out some new South Indian inspired dishes of your own!

KANCHIPURAM IDLI

Idli is a south Indian savoury cake made by steaming a batter consisting of fermented black lentils (*urad dal*) and rice. The fermentation process breaks down the starches making it easily digestible by the body.

Plain *Idlis* are popular throughout India but In this recipe the batter is flavoured with spices and vegetables and then steamed to get the kanchipuram style *Idli*.

Ingredients:

Long grain rice	2 cups
Urad dal	1 cup
Ghee	2 tablespoon
Mustard seeds	½ teaspoon
Cumin seeds	½ teaspoon
Ginger gated	¼ teaspoon
Carrot chopped	1 table spoon
Cashew nuts chopped	1 tablespoon
Curry leaves chopped	1 teaspoon
Asafoetida powder	½ teaspoon
White pepper powder	¼ teaspoon
Salt to taste	

Preparation:

1. Wash the rice and dal separately, cover with water and soak for 4 hours or overnight.

2. Drain and then grind in a blender or food processor with a little water, to form a thick and fine paste.

3. Mix with salt, cover and keep in a warm place to ferment for 8 hours or until it doubles its volume.

4. Heat ghee in a small frying pan and fry mustard seeds until they pop; add ginger, carrot, cashew nuts, curry leaves, asafoetida powder and white pepper powder, mix well. Remove from heat and leave to cool.

5. Mix the above mixture with the fermented *Idli* batter and pour into a greased round 20 cm mould or into traditional *Idli* moulds.

6. Steam cook for 20 minutes, remove from the mould (cut into pieces if using 20cm round mould). Serve hot with chutney.

MASALA DOSA

Masala dosa is made by stuffing the classic thin and crispy plain *dosa* with a dry potato curry called potato *masala*. For variation, Paneer (cottage cheese) can be used in place of the potatoes in the *masala* for filling.

POTATO MASALA

Vegetable oil	2 tablespoon
Black mustard seeds	1 teaspoon
Curry leaves	a few
Turmeric powder	½ teaspoon
Ginger grated	½ teaspoon
Green chillies chopped	1 teaspoon
Onion chopped	½ cup
Carrot chopped	½ cup
Cashew nuts	¼ cup
Green peas	¼ cup (fresh or frozen)
Salt to taste	

1. Heat the oil in a frying pan, add the mustard seeds and fry until they start to pop, add the curry leaves, turmeric, ginger, green chilli and onion. Sauté until the onions are soft.
2. Add the potatoes, carrots, cashew nuts and 250 ml of water. Bring to boil, cover and cook until the potatoes are tender and almost breaking up.
3. Add green peas and salt and simmer uncovered until all the excess water evaporates.

DOSA

Urad dal	¼ cup
Long grain rice	1 cup
Salt	1 teaspoon
Oil for cooking	

1. Wash and soak the *urad dal* and rice separately in a bowl of cold water for at least four hours or overnight.
2. Drain and grind the *dal* and rice with a little water in a food processor or blender to form a fine paste.
3. Mix the *dal* paste with the ground rice and salt. Add enough water to make a thick batter.
4. Cover and leave it in a warm place (ideally between 25 to 35 degrees Celsius) for 8 hours or until the batter ferments.

5. Heat a non-stick frying pan or a flat griddle. Lightly brush the surface of the pan with oil.
6. Stir the batter and pour a ladle full into the middle of the frying pan and spread it out to make a thin *Dosa*. Drizzle a little oil around the edge to help it crisp up.
7. Place two table spoons of the *masala* filling onto one half of the *dosa* and fold the other half over.
8. Serve with coconut *chutney* and *Sambar*.

BISI BELE BATH

This is a delicious dish of lentils, rice and vegetables cooked together with spices and tamarind to give it a hot and sour flavour. The dish originates in the state of Karnataka, with *BisiBele Bath* translating to hot lentil rice in the Kannada language. The traditional preparation of this dish is quite elaborate and time consuming. I have adapted the recipe to make it simple, using ready ground spices instead of making a spice masala, which is made by roasting and grinding *dal* and whole spices.

Serves 4-6

Ingredients:

Toor dal (yellow lentils)	100g
Basmati rice	200 g
Green peas	¼ cup
Cauliflower (cut into florets)	¼ cup
Tomato (chopped)	1 cup
Tamarind pulp	2 table spoon
Chilli powder	½ teaspoon
Turmeric powder	½ teaspoon
Asafoetida powder	½ teaspoon
Cinnamon powder	¼ teaspoon
Cardamom powder	¼ teaspoon
Cumin powder	1 teaspoon
Salt to taste	
Oil	2 table spoon
Fenugreek seeds	½ teaspoon
Mustard seeds	½ teaspoon
Dry red chilli	2
Cashew nuts (chopped)	2 table spoon
Curry leaves (chopped)	2 table spoon

Preparation:

1. Wash and cook *dal* in a saucepan with 6 cups of water until they are almost cooked.
2. Add washed rice, green peas and cauliflower and simmer for ten minutes, stir occasionally.
3. Add the tomato, tamarind pulp, all the spice powders and salt. Simmer gently until the lentils and rice are cooked and has a porridge like consistency.
4. Heat oil in a small frying pan and fry fenugreek seeds and mustard seeds until thy pop. Add dry chilli cut into half, cashew nuts and curry leaves and fry till cashew nuts are golden brown.
5. Pour the above mixture over the lentil-rice mixture, mix well and serve with *poppadums*.

ONION UTAPPAM

Utappam is a thick pancake made with fermented rice and black lentil (*urad dal*) *dosa* batter, which is a very popular breakfast and dinner staple. Chopped onions are mixed into the batter in this version to add flavour and texture into the classic simple *dosa*. It is often eaten with *sambar* or *chutney.*

Ingredients:

Urad dal	¼ cup
Long grain rice	1 cup
Or	
Rice flour	1 cups
Salt	1 teaspoon
Onion chopped	1 cup
Green chilli chopped	1 teaspoon
Oil for frying	

Preparation:

1. Wash and soak *urad dal* and rice separately in cold water for 4 to 6 hours.
2. Grind soaked *dal* and rice in a food processor or blender to make a fine thick batter (if using rice flour mix with water to make a thick batter).
3. Mix both the batters together with salt, cover and keep in a warm place (ideally between 20 to 30 degrees Celsius) for 8 hours or overnight until it ferments.
4. Mix with chopped onion and green chilli, add more water if needed to make a thick pancake like batter.
5. Heat a non-stick frying pan or a flat griddle, brush with oil and pour a ladle full of batter and spread it to make a thick pancake.
6. Once tiny holes appear on the pancake sprinkle some oil around the *Utappam* and on top.
7. Flip it over to the other side and cook till both sides are slightly browned and cooked.
8. Serve with *Sambar* or chutney while still hot.

PULIYOGARE (TAMARIND RICE)

This is a spicy and tangy rice dish ideal for picnics and travels. Sesame oil is used in this recipe to give an extra flavour. The tamarind sauce can be made in big batches and stored in an airtight container in the fridge for almost a month for future use.

Ingredients:

Long grain rice	2 cups
Water	3 cups
Salt	½ teaspoon
Tamarind	lime size ball
Sesame oil	2 table spoon
Mustard seeds	½ teaspoon
Cumin seeds	½ teaspoon
Chilli powder	¼ teaspoon
Coriander powder	¼ teaspoon
Turmeric powder	¼ teaspoon
Asafoetida powder	¼ teaspoon
Curry leaves	a few
Brown sugar	2 table spoon
Salt to taste	
Roasted peanuts	2 table spoon
Sesame seeds	1 table spoon

Preparation:

1. Wash and cook rice in 3 cups of water and salt until all the water is absorbed, keep aside.
2. Soak tamarind in one cup of hot water for ten minutes, extract the juice and sieve.
3. Heat oil in a wok or frying pan, add mustard seeds and cumin seeds and fry until they pop. Add chilli powder, coriander powder, Turmeric powder, asafoetida powder and curry leaves, sauté on low heat for a minute until fragrant.
4. Add brown sugar, tamarind pulp and salt, boil together until you get a thick tamarind sauce.
5. Mix the cooked rice with tamarind sauce, roasted peanuts and sesame seeds. Serve with fried *poppadums*.

VEGETABLE RAVA UPUMA

Upuma is a typical south Indian breakfast dish made with coarse semolina, which is popularly known as *rava* in South India. Variations of flavours and ingredients in *upuma* can be found in different southern states. This recipe is my favourite with lots of vegetables and cashew nuts for texture. Coarse semolina can be substituted with coarse polenta or couscous.

Ingredients:

Oil	2 tablespoon
Mustard seeds	½ teaspoon
Onion (chopped)	¼ cup
Ginger (chopped)	½ teaspoon
Green chilli (chopped)	½ teaspoon
Curry leaves	a few
Carrot (chopped)	¼ cup
Green peas	¼ cup
Cashew nuts(chopped)	3 table spoon
Coarse semolina	1 cup
Hot water	1½ cup
Salt to taste	
Ghee	1 table spoon

Preparation:

1. Heat the oil in a wok or saucepan and fry mustard seeds until they pop. Add onion, ginger, green chilli, curry leaves and chopped carrot. Sauté until onions are soft.
2. Add green peas, cashew nuts and semolina, sauté for a few minutes until the semolina is roasted well and coated with oil.
3. Add hot water and salt, cover and cook until all the water is absorbed. Add ghee to finish, mix well and serve hot.

PLAIN DOSA

These are thin, spongy rice pancakes with a crisp surface. They are traditionally eaten with *Sambar* (spicy lentil stew) or with coconut *chutney* for breakfast. But if you have the batter ready in the fridge it can be served as a delicious quick lunch, dinner or snack.

Ingredients:

Urad dal	¼ cup
Long grain rice	1 cups
Salt	1 teaspoon
Oil for cooking	

Preparation:

1. Wash and soak the *urad dal* and rice separately in a bowl of cold water for at least four hours or overnight.
2. Drain and grind the *dal* and rice separately with a little water in a food processor or blender to form a fine paste.
3. Mix the *dal* paste and ground rice with salt and add enough water to make a thick batter.
4. Cover and leave it in a warm place for 8 hours or until the batter ferments and doubles.
5. Heat a non-stick frying pan or a flat griddle over medium heat, lightly brush the surface with oil.
6. Stir the batter and pour ladlefull into the middle of the frying pan and spread it out to make a thin *Dosa*. Drizzle a little oil around the edge to help it crisp up.
7. Cook until small holes appear on the surface, turn over with a spatula and cook the other side.
8. Serve with *Sambar* or *chutney*.

COCONUT CHUTNEY (KERALA STYLE)

This *chutney* is made with fresh grated coconut all over south India, It is very simple to make and usually served with *Dosas* or *Iddlis* for breakfast.

Grated fresh coconut	½ cup
Green chilli	2
Shallots	2-3
Curry leaves	a few
Ginger	(chopped) ½ teaspoon
Yogurt	1 table spoon
Oil	1 table spoon
Mustard seeds	1 teaspoon
Dry red chilli	1
Salt to taste	

1. Grind together coconut, green chilli, shallots, curry leaves, ginger, yogurt and salt in a blender with half cup of water to a coarse texture.
2. Heat oil in a small frying pan and fry mustard seeds until they pop add red chilli cut into half and fry until light brown in colour, add curry leaves and pour over *chutney* and mix well.

KOTHAMALLI CHUTNEY (CORIANDER CHUTNEY)

This *chutney* uses lots of fresh coriander leaves which gives it a bright green colour. It can be stored in the fridge for a couple of days in an airtight container. Serve with *Idli, Dosa, Utappam* or as a filling for a delicious *chutney* sandwich for a packed lunch. If fresh grated coconut is not available use desiccated coconut instead, add two table spoons of extra water when blending together.

Fresh coriander leaves	½ cup (chopped)
Grated coconut	`½ cup
Green chilli (chopped)	`½ teaspoon
Ginger chopped	`¼ teaspoon
Garlic chopped	`¼ teaspoon
Plain yogurt	`2 table spoon
Sugar	`1 teaspoon
Salt to taste	

1. Blend all the ingredients in a food processor or blender to make a coarse paste. Add water if necessary to make a thick *chutney*.
2. Adjust the seasoning and serve cold or room at temperature.

THAKKALI CHUTNEY (TOMATO CHUTNEY)

In India *chutneys* are a semi solid paste made of a combination of fresh ingredients ground together. In this *chutney* fried *urad dal*, onions and ripe tomatoes are ground together with spices to make a fresh *chutney* which can be served with *dosa, idli*, or as a spread for sandwiches.

Oil	1 table spoon
Urad dal	2 table spoon
Onion (chopped)	¼ cup
Curry leaves	a few
Chilli powder	½ teaspoon
Asafoetida powder	¼ teaspoon
Ginger (chopped)	¼ teaspoon
Tomato (chopped)	1 cup

1. Fry the *urad dal* in oil until it is lightly golden brown. Add onion and sauté until they are soft.
2. Add curry leaves chilli powder, asafoetida powder and ginger, sauté for a minute until fragrant.
3. Blend the above mixture with chopped tomatoes and salt to a fine paste in a blender or food processor.

SAMBAR

Sambar is an example of the ancient tradition of *dal*-based vegetable stews in South India. It is a vegetable stew made with a lentil (*toor dal*) and tamarind based broth. It is mostly served with plain rice, *Idli* or with *Dosa*. Each state of south India prepares it with a typical variation, adapted to its culture and taste. A spice mixture called *sambar* powder is mostly used these days and its available in the Indian grocery stores but I like to use individual spice powders lightly toasted in oil but if you prefer to use *sambar* powder just substitute the spice powders and adjust the seasoning. The amount of spices used in this recipe gives a very mild flavoured finish to the dish but if you prefer a spicy broth double the amount of Chilli powder used in this recipe. A wide variety of vegetables can be added to Sambar according to your preference. The popular ones are aubergine, carrots, drumsticks, okra, radish, Pumpkin, french beans etc.

Ingredients:

Toor dal (yellow lentils)	¼ cup
Onion	1
Tomato	1
Potato	1
Pumpkin	100g
Okra	100 g
Tamarind pulp	2 table spoon
Oil	1 table spoon
Mustard seeds	1 tea spoon
Curry leaves	a few
Chilli powder	½ tea spoon
Coriander powder	1 tea spoon
Turmeric powder	¼ tea spoon
Asafoetida powder	½ tea spoon
Coriander leaves (chopped)	2 table spoons
Salt	

Preparation:

1. Wash *toor dal* and cook with chopped onions, chopped tomato and two cups of water until the dal is cooked.
2. Add diced potato and cook till they are starting to get soft, add diced pumpkin and okra cut into small pieces, simmer till vegetables are tender.
3. Add the tamarind pulp and salt, boil and keep aside.
4. Heat oil in a small saucepan and fry mustard seeds until they start to pop, add curry leaves and remove from heat then add all the spice powders and mix well. Pour into the cooked vegetable and *dal* mixture and simmer for a few minutes.
5. Check for seasoning and add chopped coriander leaves to finish.

VEGETABLE BIRYANI

Biryani is originally from Iran (Persia) and was brought to South India by Arab spice merchants. The rice is cooked separately and mixed with a curry of vegetables and then cooked together resulting in a rice with hint of aromas and flavours of vegetable curry.

Ingredients:

Basmati rice	2 cups
Water	4 cups
Ghee	2 tablespoons
Oil	4 tablespoons
Sliced onion	1 cup
Green chilli chopped	1 tablespoon
Ginger (grated)	1 teaspoon
Garlic (grated)	1 teaspoon
Chilli powder	½ teaspoon
Turmeric powder	½ teaspoon
Garam masala	2 teaspoons
Tomato (chopped)	½ cup
Plain yogurt	½ cup
Baby corn (cut into 1 cm pieces)	½ cup
Carrot (cut onto 1 cm cubes)	½ cup
Cauliflower (cut into florets)	½ cup
Green peas	½ cup
Cashew nuts	¼ cup
Salt to taste	
Coriander and mint leaves chopped-	¼ cup
Fried onions to garnish	

Preparation:

1. Wash the rice and cook in a saucepan with ½ tea spoon of salt and4 cups of water until all the water is absorbed.
2. Mix with ghee and keep aside.
3. Heat oil in a large saucepan and sauté the onions until they turn golden brown, add ginger, garlic and green chilli and sauté till fragrant.
4. Add chilli powder, turmeric powder and garam *masala*. Sauté for a minute, then add chopped tomato, plain yogurt, vegetables, cashew nuts and salt to taste. Cover and cook until vegetables are cooked.
5. Into the bottom of an ovenproof dish, layer 1/3 of the cooked rice. Layer on top with half the curry, then sprinkle the chopped coriander and mint on top of the curry layer.
6. Repeat this layering process, finishing off with the last 1/3 layer of rice.
7. Cover with a tight lid and cook on a very low flame for 15 minutes or bake in medium hot oven for 15 to 20 minutes.
8. Serve garnished with fried onions, chopped coriander and a drizzle of ghee.

VELLARIKAI, THAKKALI, VENGAYA PACHADI
(CUCUMBER, TOMATO AND ONION - YOGURT SALAD)

This is a simple yogurt based salad with aromatic oil poured over to give a delicious finish. I have used a mixture of all three vegetables here but for a distinct flavour you can use any one of these vegetables instead of all three mixed together.

Ingredients:

Cucumber (peeled and chopped)	½
Tomato (chopped)	1
Red onion (peeled and chopped)	1
Plain yogurt	1 cup
Oil	1 tablespoon
Mustard seeds	1 teaspoon
Dry red chilli	1
Asafoetida powder	¼ teaspoon
Curry leaves	a few
Salt to taste	

Preparation:

1. Mix the cucumber, tomato and onion with salt and yogurt and keep aside.

2. Heat oil in a small frying pan and fry mustard seeds until they pop, add dry red chilli cut into half and fry until light brown in colour. Remove from heat add asafoetida powder and curry leaves, mix well, pour over the vegetable and yogurt mixture and combine together.

3. Serve cold or at room temperature.

VERMICELLI WITH RICE AND COCONUT

Ingredients:

Basmati rice	100 g
Vermicelli	100 g
Water	1 cup
Salt	¼ teaspoon
Butter	1 table spoon
Oil	2 table spoon
Mustard seeds	½ teaspoon
Dry red chilli	1
Curry leaves	a few
Green chilli (chopped)	½ teaspoon
Ginger (chopped)	½ teaspoon
Cashew nuts	¼ cup
Hot water	1 cup
Grated coconut	½ cup
Salt to taste	

Coriander leaves and fried onions to garnish

Preparation:

1. Wash rice and cook with 1 cup of water and salt until all the water is absorbed, fluff with a fork and mix with butter and keep aside.
2. Heat oil and fry mustard seeds until they pop, add dry chilli and sauté until it is slightly browned. Add curry leaves, green chilli and ginger, sauté for a minute.
3. Add vermicelli and cashew nut, sauté until all the vermicelli is coated with spices and oil.
4. Add 1 cup of hot water and salt, cook until vermicelli is cooked and all the water is absorbed.
5. Mix with the cooked rice and grated coconut. Serve garnished with coriander leaves and fried onions

BEETROOT CURRY IN COCONUT MILK

This is an interesting curry with the sweetness of beetroot and coconut milk. The bright pink colour from the beetroot makes it a very exotic and attractive dish.

Ingredients:

Oil	2 table spoon
Mustard seeds	1 teaspoon
Curry leaves	a few
Onion (sliced)	½ cup
Garlic (chopped)	1 teaspoon
Beetroot	250 g
Chilli powder	½ teaspoon
Coriander powder	1 teaspoon
Turmeric powder	¼ teaspoon
Thick coconut milk	1 cup
Salt to taste	

Preparation:

1. Peel and cut beetroot into thin long matchstick strips.
2. Heat oil in a wok or saucepan and fry mustard seeds until they pop, add curry leaves, onion and garlic, sauté until onions are tender.
3. Add the beetroot and sauté for a few minutes and then add chilli powder, coriander powder and turmeric powder, sauté till fragrant.
4. Add ½ cup of water and salt, cover and cook on low heat until the beetroot is cooked through.
5. Add coconut milk and bring to boil. Serve with plain rice or with bread.

BABY CORN AND CARROT STIR FRY

This stir fry is surprisingly easy to make and delicious served with any kind of food from around the world.

Ingredients:

Ghee	1 table spoon
Cumin seeds	1 teaspoon
Ginger grated	½ teaspoon
Garlic grated	½ teaspoon
Chilli powder	¼ teaspoon
Crushed cardamom	¼ teaspoon
Tomato (chopped)	¼ cup
Baby corn	200 g
Carrot	100 g
Onion (cut into wedges)	100 g
Salt to taste	
Coriander leaves	

Preparation:

1. Cut baby corn lengthwise into half. Cut carrot into long sticks (same size as corn)

2. Heat ghee and fry cumin seeds until they are fragrant, add ginger, garlic, chilli powder, crushed cardamom and chopped tomato, sauté for a minute

3. Add baby corn, carrots, onions and salt, cover and cook till vegetables are cooked but crunchy.

4. Serve garnished with coriander leaves.

MIXED VEGETABLE KOOTU

Kootu is a traditional vegetable dish with vegetables and pulses cooked together and flavoured with ground coconut and spices. Every state in south India has their own traditional version depending on the pulses, spices and vegetable combinations used. This is my simple version with mixed vegetables and chickpeas, a perfect side dish for rice or chapati bread. If fresh grated coconut is not available use half the quantity of desiccated coconut instead. Cooked chickpeas can be substituted with any kind of canned beans (brown lentils and pigeon peas etc.)

Ingredients:

Cooked chick peas	1 cup
Mixed vegetables	3 cups
(Potato, carrot, cauliflower, green peas)	
Salt to taste	
Grated coconut	½ cup
Chilli powder	1 teaspoon
Coriander powder	1 teaspoon
Cumin seeds	½ teaspoon
Turmeric powder	½ teaspoon
Shallots	2
Oil	1 table spoon
Mustard seeds	1 teaspoon
Dry chilli	2
Grated coconut	1 table spoon
Curry leaves	a few

Preparation:

1. Coarsely chop the carrots, cauliflower and potato . Cook with chickpeas until the vegetables are tender, add green peas and cook for a few minutes.
2. Grind together grated coconut, chilli powder, coriander powder, cumin seeds, turmeric powder and shallots in a blender adding enough water to make a fine paste.
3. Add salt and the ground coconut paste to the cooked vegetables. Simmer for a few minutes.
4. Heat oil and fry mustard seeds until fragrant, add dry chilli and coconut, fry until coconut is light brown in colour and then add curry leaves and pour over cooked *kootu.* Mix lightly before serving.

PARIPPU CURRY (Dal curry)

Parippu curry is an essential part of the traditional vegetarian feast (*sadya*) in Kerala. It is usually served with plain hot rice, ghee and *poppadums* as the first course for wedding and festival meals.

This curry is mild and light and is always loved by adults as well as children. *Mung dal* can be substituted with *toor dal* and if fresh coconut is not available use half the quantity of desiccated coconut instead.

Ingredients:

Mung dal	½ cup
Water	2 cups
Grated coconut	¼ cup
Shallot	1
Green chilli	1
Coriander powder	½ teaspoon
Turmeric powder	½ teaspoon
Oil	1 table spoon
Mustard seeds	½ teaspoon
Dry chilli	1
Curry leaves	a few
Salt to taste	

Preparation:

1. Wash and cook (simmer gently) dal with 2 cups of water until tender and the dal starts to break down.

2. Grind together grated coconut, shallot, green chilli, coriander powder and turmeric powder in a blender to make a fine paste, adding water if necessary.

3. Add the ground ingredients to the cooked *dal* and heat till it starts to boil. Keep aside.

4. Heat oil and fry mustard seeds until they pop and are fragrant, add dry chilli cut into half and curry leaves, Fry until dry chilli is light brown in colour. Pour over the cooked *dal* mixture, add salt and mix well. Serve with plain rice.

Mung dal

Sadya

OKRA MASALA

Okra or ladies finger is cooked in different ways in India.
This recipe is one of my favourites. It is so easy to prepare and is a perfect accompaniment for a quick meal or as a side dish for a dinner party.

Ingredients:

Ghee	1½ tablespoon
Onion (Chopped)	½ cup
Ginger(chopped)	½ teaspoon
Chilli powder	½ teaspoon
Coriander powder	½ teaspoon
Turmeric powder	¼ teaspoon
Garam *masala*	½ teaspoon
Okra	250 g
Tomato	1
Coriander leaves (chopped)	1 tablespoon
Salt to taste	

Preparation:

1. Heat ghee and sauté chopped onion and ginger until onions are tender.
2. Add chilli powder, coriander powder, turmeric powder and *garam masala*, sauté on a low heat for a minute until the spices are fragrant.
3. Add okra cut into 1 cm pieces and sauté until cooked.
4. Add salt, tomato cut into small pieces and chopped coriander. Mix well and serve hot.

Garam Masala

To grind to fine powder to make *garam masala
½ teaspoon cardamom
½ teaspoon cloves
½ teaspoon fennel
2 sprigs curry leaves

PACHAKKARI THORAN

Thoran is a dry vegetable dish, which is flavoured with mustard seeds, curry leaves and fresh grated coconut. It is an indispensable part of Kerala cuisine and is made with many different kinds of vegetables.
I have used a combination of cabbage, carrots and French beans in this recipe but you can make it with other individual vegetables as well. Use ¼ cup of desiccated coconut if fresh grated coconut is not available.

Ingredients:

Oil	1 tablespoon
Mustard seeds	1 teaspoon
Dry chilli	1
Green chilli chopped	½ teaspoon
Cabbage chopped	1 cup
Carrot chopped	½ cup
French beans chopped	½ cup
Grated coconut	½ cup
Turmeric powder	½ teaspoon
Salt to taste	

Preparation:

1. Heat the oil in a wok or frying pan and fry mustard seeds until they pop and are fragrant, add dry chilli cut into half and curry leaves and fry till fragrant.
2. Add all the other ingredients to this mixture and mix well, cover and cook on low heat for ten minutes or until the vegetables are cooked.

RADISH AND COCONUT SALAD (KOSAMBRI)

Kosambri is a salad like dish from Mysore. In this recipe I have used a combination of red radishes, *dal* and grated coconut but there are many variations and you can use coarsely grated carrots, chopped dycon radishes or diced cucumbers instead of red radishes. Substitute the *mung dal* with chopped salted peanuts for an interesting crunchy texture.

Ingredients:

Small radish (one bunch)	250 g
Oil	2 tablespoon
Mustard seeds	1 teaspoon
Dried chilli	2
Mung dal	2 tablespoon
Curry leaves	a few
Grated fresh coconut	¼ cup
Lime or lemon juice	1/ 2 tablespoon
Salt	to taste

Preparation:

1. Wash and quarter the radishes.
2. Heat oil and fry the mustard seeds until they pop, add the dry chilli, curry leaves and *mung dal*, fry until the *dal* turns a golden colour. Remove from the heat and add lime or lemon juice.
3. Add the grated coconut, salt and the quartered radishes, toss well and serve.

OKRA MORU CURRY (OKRA MASALA PACHADI)

Okra, which is more commonly known as ladies fingers or *vendeka* in South India, is found in abundance throughout India. When buying okra, be careful to ensure that they are small, bright green in colour, crisp and firm. Fried okra has a special nutty flavour, which goes well with the yogurt. This dish serves as an excellent side dish for any rice preparation or with Indian breads.

Ingredients:

Okra (sliced thin)	200 g
Oil	5 table spoon
Fenugreek seeds	¼ teaspoon
Mustard seeds	1 teaspoon
Dry red chilli	2
Curry leaves	a few
Onion chopped	½ cup
Ginger chopped	½ teaspoon
Turmeric powder	¼ teaspoon
Tomato chopped	½ cup
Salt	to taste
Yogurt	1 cup

Preparation:

1. Heat 4 tablespoons of oil and fry thinly sliced okra until brown and crisp, remove and keep aside.

2. Heat the rest of the oil in a wok or sauce pan and fry fenugreek seeds and mustard seeds until fragrant, add dry chilli cut into small pieces and curry leaves and fry until dry chilli is light brown in colour.

3. Add onion and ginger and sauté until onions are tender, add turmeric powder, chopped tomato and salt. Remove from the heat and mix with fried Okra and yogurt. Check for seasoning and serve.

SHALLOTS AND GREEN BANANA THEYAL

This is a very popular dish from central Kerala. Grated coconut is roasted with spices and ground to a fine paste for the spicy and nutty curry sauce. I like to serve it with plain rice and fried *pappodams*.

Ingredients:

Vegetable oil	2 tablespoon
Mustard seeds	½ teaspoon
Curry leaves	10
Green banana or plantain	200 g
Shallots	200 g
Tomato quartered	½ cup
Tamarind pulp	1 tablespoon
Salt	
Fresh grated coconut	½ cup
Garlic	1 clove
Curry leaves	10
Chilli powder	1 teaspoon
Coriander powder	½ teaspoon
Turmeric powder	½ teaspoon

Preparation:

1. Dry roast grated coconut with sliced garlic and curry leaves till coconut turns brown, reduce the heat and add chilli powder, coriander powder and turmeric powder, sauté for a minute until the mixture is fragrant and brown. Remove from heat and allow to cool.
2. Grind the roasted coconut mixture to a fine paste using a spice mill or blender. Add water to get a fine paste.
3. Peel and slice banana into 1cm thick slices, peel and halve the shallots.
4. Heat oil in a saucepan or wok and fry mustard seeds until they pop, add curry leaves, green banana pieces and shallots and sauté for a few minutes.
5. Add tomato, the spice paste, salt and enough water to make a curry sauce. Cover and cook till the bananas are soft, add tamarind pulp and check the seasoning adding more salt if necessary.

This curry can be made with any chunky vegetable. Asian shallots are used in this recipe but can be easily substituted with Baby onions or banana shallots Fresh grated coconut can be substituted with desiccated coconut and tamarind pulp with lemon or lime juice.

SPICY NEW POTATOES WITH SPINACH

New potatoes and baby leaf spinach are wonderful ingredients, whose flavours compliment each other in this delicious dish. I like to serve this simple home style preparation with *Chapatis* or with *Puris* for a casual home meal.

Ingredients:

Small new potatoes	250 g
Vegetable oil	2 tablespoon
Mustard seeds	½ teaspoon
Onion chopped	½ cup
Ginger chopped	½ teaspoon
Garlic chopped	½ teaspoon
Chilli powder	½ teaspoon
Turmeric powder	½ teaspoon
Garam masala	½ teaspoon
Tomatoes chopped	½ cup
Baby leaf spinach	250 g
Lemon juice	½ tablespoon
Salt to taste	

Preparation:

1. Place the new potatoes in a large saucepan, add ½ teaspoon of salt, cover with cold water and cook until the potatoes are tender. Drain, peel and set aside.

2. Heat the oil in a large frying pan, add the mustard seeds and when they start to pop add onion, ginger and garlic. Sauté until the onions are tender, add the chilli powder, turmeric powder and *garam masala*, sauté for a minute.

3. Add chopped tomato and salt and cook till tomatoes are tender and falling apart. Then add the spinach and cook until they are wilted, add the boiled new potatoes and lemon juice, mix well and cook till all the water is evaporated. Serve hot.

THAKKALI KOTHAMALLI RASAM
(Tomato and Coriander *Rasam*)

Rasam is a traditional spicy soup, made with tamarind pulp, tomato and a mixture of other spices. Nowadays, a special ready made *Rasam* Powder is readily available in Indian grocery stores, however, I find that to give it maximum flavour, it should be made from scratch with fresh spices. In south India people complement it with plain rice for a light meal, any time of the day. Taking only 10 to 15 minutes to prepare, this recipe is a perfect starter for the winter months.

Ingredients:

Cumin seeds	½ teaspoon
Pepper corns	½ teaspoon
Garlic (chopped)	`½ teaspoon
Ghee	1tablespoon
Mustard seeds	½ teaspoon
Chilli powder	½ teaspoon
Coriander powder	`1 teaspoon
Turmeric powder	`¼ teaspoon
Asafoetida powder	`½ teaspoon
Tomato chopped	`¼ cup
Tamarind pulp	1 tablespoon
Water	500ml
Coriander leaves chopped	`¼ cup
Salt to taste	

Preparation:

1. Crush cumin seeds, peppercorns and garlic together in a pestle and mortar and keep aside.
2. Heat ghee in a saucepan and fry mustard seeds until they pop, add crushed ingredients and sauté until fragrant.
3. Add chilli powder, coriander powder, turmeric powder and asafoetida and sauté on low heat and add tomato, tamarind pulp and water. Cook covered for ten to fifteen minutes.
4. Add coriander leaves and salt to finish.

VEGETABLE BHAJI (Mixed Vegetable Fritters)

These deep fried mixed vegetable fritters make an excellent starter or snack. The batter is made from chickpea flour, known as besan or gram flour in India. Rice flour is added to the batter for crispiness, however if you can't get rice flour, this can be left out. These *bhajis* taste excellent when served piping hot but if you want to prepare them ahead, fry them lightly beforehand and then refry till golden and crispy just before serving.

Ingredients:

Chick pea flour (Besan)	200 g
Rice flour (optional)	2 table spoon
Chilli powder	1 teaspoon
Turmeric powder	¼ teaspoon
Asafoetida powder	¼ teaspoon
Salt	1 teaspoon
Onion	1
Carrot	1
Green pepper	1
Aubergine	1
Curry leaves	2 table spoon
Oil for deep frying	

Preparation:

1. Cut the onion, carrot, green pepper and aubergine into thin strips.
2. Mix together the chickpea flour, rice flour, chilli powder, turmeric powder, asafoetida powder and salt. Add enough water to make a thick batter, which will hold the vegetables together.
3. Mix the vegetables and curry leaves into the batter.
4. Heat the oil in a saucepan or wok and deep fry a spoonful of the vegetable mixture in hot oil until crispy and golden brown.

You can use practically any vegetable combinations for mixed bhajis. Instead of mixing the vegetables you can also dip individual pieces of vegetables in the batter and deep fry.

VENGAYA BHAJI (ONION FRITTERS)

These onion fritters are surprisingly easy to make and this is always a family favourite loved by adults as well as children. It freezes well and for dinner parties I make it ahead and warm it in the oven or refry just before serving.

Ingredients:

Onion (thinly sliced)	2 cups
Curry leaves	¼ cup
Asafoetida powder	¼ teaspoon
Chilli powder	½ teaspoon
Turmeric powder	¼ teaspoon
Salt	½ teaspoon
Water	2 table spoon
Besan (chickpea flour)	1 cup
Rice flour	2 table spoon
Oil for deep frying	

Preparation:

1. Combine all the ingredients except oil for frying in a bowl, leave aside for 10 minutes. Add a little water and mix well until it becomes a wet and stiff mixture.

2. Heat oil in a deep frying pan and drop a spoonfull of mixture into the hot oil, fry until golden brown and crisp.

3. Drain on kitchen paper to absorb excess oil. Serve hot with drinks or as a starter or with tea or coffee for snack.

BEETROOT CUTLETS

This is the Indian version of French potato croquets coated in bread crumbs and deep-fried. Beetroot cutlets can be served as a starter, however in India it is mostly served as a teatime snack. These cutlets can be made ahead and can be frozen for a few weeks. Thaw them in the fridge for a few hours before deep-frying.

Ingredients:

Oil	2 table spoon
Mustard seeds	1 teaspoon
Curry leaves (chopped)	a few
Ginger chopped	½ teaspoon
Onion chopped	½ cup
Chilli powder	½ teaspoon
Turmeric powder	½ teaspoon
Garam masala	1 teaspoon
Beet root (cooked)	150 g
Potato	150 g
Green peas	½ cup
Salt	to taste
Oil for deep frying	

Coating

Egg	1
Bread crumbs	½ cup

Preparation:

1. Heat oil and fry mustard seeds until they pop, add curry leaves, ginger and onion, sauté until onions are tender.
2. Add chilli powder, turmeric powder and *garam masala*, sauté on low heat until fragrant.
3. Add diced potato, chopped beetroot, green peas and half-cup of water. Cover and cook until potatoes and beetroots are tender and all the water has evaporated.
4. Season with salt, cool and mash with a fork. Shape them into small ovals, about 5cm long.
5. Dip them in beaten egg and then coat with breadcrumbs. Deep fry in hot oil till golden brown. Serve with tomato *chutney* or chilli sauce.

MASALA VADA

This deep fried snack from South India is a distant cousin of the falafel from the Middle East. These delightful morsels are an excellent starter for any party or perfect as snacks for the kids after a tiring day at school. You can use split peas or red lentils instead of *channa dal.*

Shallots can be substituted with white or red onions and curry leaves with coriander leaves or parsley.

Ingredients:

Channa dal (split chickpeas)	1 cup
Shallots chopped	2 tablespoon
Ginger chopped	1 teaspoon
Curry leaves chopped	2 tablespoon
Chilli powder	1 teaspoon
Salt	1 teaspoon
Oil for deep frying	

Preparation:

1. Wash and soak the *channa dal* in cold water for three to four hours and drain.
2. Coarsely grind the soaked and drained *dal* in a food processor [or in a large pestle and mortar if you have one]. Add the shallots, ginger, curry leaves, and chilli powder, mix well and season with salt.
3. Shape into golf ball sized balls and slightly flatten each ball to form a patty.
4. Deep-fry the patties in hot oil until golden brown and crisp. Drain well on paper towels and serve hot.

MASALA KOZHUKKATTA
(SAVOURY RICE DUMPLINGS)

Kozhukkattais a speciality of Kerala state. Traditionally it is made with a sweet filling using grated coconut and brown sugar. This savoury version is perfect for people who don't have a sweet tooth.

Ingredients:

Rice flour	1 cup
Salt	¼ teaspoon
Hot water	1 cup
Oil	2 table spoon
Mustard seeds	½ teaspoon
Curry leaves (chopped)	1 table spoon
Onion (chopped)	1 cup
Chilli powder	½ teaspoon
Garam masala	1 teaspoon
Turmeric powder	¼ teaspoon
Tomato chopped	½ cup
Sweet corn kernels	¼ cup
Green peas	¼ cup
Salt to taste	

If corn kernels are hard to find use chopped cashew nuts instead. Chopped boiled egg works extremely well too.

Preparation:

1. Place the rice flour and salt in a big bowl, pour hot water in and mix with wooden spoon or spatula until it clumps together.

2. Cool down slightly and knead with wet hands until you get a soft but firm dough. Make golf sized balls and keep aside.

3. To make the filling, heat oil and fry mustard seeds until they pop and then add curry leaves and chopped onion and sauté till tender.

4. Add chilli powder, *Garam masala* and turmeric powder, sauté on a low heat until fragrant.

5. Then add chopped tomato, sweet corn kernels, green peas and salt to taste. Cover and cook on a low heat until everything is cooked together. Cool and keep aside.

6. Flatten the rice dough balls slightly using your finger tips, keep a spoonful of filling in the middle, fold the dough around the filling and seal the top to make a smooth ball.

7. Boil water in a steamer and steam the filled *kozhukkatas* for 15 to 20 minutes on medium heat.

RAVA KESARI

Rava kesari is a traditional speciality of south India. It can be prepared in minutes with simple ingredients. A perfect dessert when paired with summer fruits or with mangoes.

Ingredients:

Milk	1½ cups
Sugar	1 cup
Coarse semolina	1 cup
Ghee	4 table spoon
Cardamom powder	¼ teaspoon
Cashew nuts	1 table spoon
Raisins	1 table spoon

Preparation:

1. Boil together milk and sugar in a saucepan.
2. Heat ghee in another saucepan and fry semolina, chopped cashew nuts and raisins lightly for a few minutes.
3. Add cardamom powder and hot milk and sugar mixture. Cook over low heat stirring all the time, until all the liquid is absorbed.
4. Transfer to a greased plate and spread to one inch thickness. When cool cut into diamond shapes and serve.

PARIPPU PAYASAM

Payasam is served at the end of almost all wedding feasts and festival meals in Kerala. The traditional method of preparing this dish is time consuming, but if you use powdered brown sugar and canned coconut milk it's an incredibly easy dish to prepare in any kitchen. You can use channa dal instead of mung dal or a mixture of both.

Ingredients:

Mung dal	½ cup
Water	4 cups
Brown sugar	1 cup
Coconut milk	500 ml
Ginger powder	½ teaspoon
Cardamom powder	½ teaspoon
Ghee	1 table spoon
Cashew nuts	2 table spoon

Preparation:

1. Wash and cook *mung dal* in four cups of water until it is soft and almost starts to break down.

2. Add brown sugar and coconut milk, simmer gently until you get a thick porridge - like consistency. Remove from heat, add ginger powder and cardamom powder, mix well and keep aside.

3. Heat ghee and fry cashew nuts until golden, pour over the cooked *payasam* and mix well. Serve hot or at room temperature.

PANCHAMRUTHAM

Indians are deeply religious people they believe that foods are gifts from the Gods. *Prasadam* or holy food is offered in Hindu temples as special dishes to thank God. Desserts or sweets are the most commonly offered *Prasadam* in places of worship. *Panchamrutham* is a fruit based sweet made in Palani temple in Tamil Nadu and served as *prasadam.* A mixture of bananas and plantains are used in this recipe, if plantains are not available use an extra banana instead.

Ingredients:

Ghee	2 table spoon
Banana (cut into cubes)	1
Plantain(cut into cubes)	1
Cashew nuts	50 g
Dates	50 g
Raisins	50 g
Brown sugar	50 g
Honey	1 table spoon
Cardamom powder	½ teaspoon

Preparation:

1. Heat ghee and fry banana and plantain cubes until brown all around, add cashew nuts, chopped dates, raisins and brown sugar, cook for ten minutes on low heat until everything is well mixed and cooked together.

2. Add honey and cardamom powder to finish, mix well and allow cool.

COCONUT LADOO

Sweets are the essential part of Indian celebrations and festivals. These coconut sweets are very easy to make and only require simple ingredients that can be found in most grocery stores. It tastes delicious when made with freshly grated coconut but if it is hard to find use desiccated coconut instead. It reminds me of my birthdays during childhood when my mother used to make big batches of this, however it never lasted till the guests came around.

Makes 10

Ingredients:

Sugar	½ cup
Milk	1 cup
Grated fresh coconut	1½ cups
or	
Desiccated coconut	1cup
Cardamom powder	¼ teaspoon
Butter	2 table spoon

Preparation:

1. Boil together sugar, milk and coconut until all the liquid is evaporated, add cardamom powder and butter and mix well.
2. Cool slightly and make small lime sized balls of radius 2.5cm.

Publish and Sell your books Worldwide !

DEE BEE BOOKS has got the expertise and experience in designing, printing,
publishing and marketing books of quality, clearly depicting the concept of the subjects dealt with.
The Cook Books and Picture Books published by them have a degree of excellence
on par with world publications.
The right place for you to publish and sell worldwide.

More information:
salimpushpanath@gmail.com

A leading provider of images in digital services
We focus on producing the most effective and attractive images.

www.salimpushpanath.com